CAMBRIDGESHIRE LIBRARIES
PETERBOROUGH DIVISION
SCHOOL LIBRARY SERVICE

A FIRST LOOK BOOK

Military Planes

David Jefferis

Franklin Watts
London New York Toronto Sydney

© 1985 Franklin Watts Ltd

First published in Great Britain
   1985 by
Franklin Watts Ltd
12a Golden Square
London W1

First published in the USA by
Franklin Watts Inc.
387 Park Avenue South
New York
N.Y. 10016

UK ISBN: 0 86313 218 9
US ISBN: 0-531-04944-2
Library of Congress Catalog Card
   Number: 84-51998

Photographs supplied by
British Aerospace
Grumman Corp., NY
David Jefferis
Lockheed Corporation, Georgia
MARS, Lincs
MOD (RAF)/Sgt. J. Chance
US Air Force
US Navy

Illustrated by
Michael Roffe
Hayward Art Group

Technical consultant
Mark Hewish

Printed in Great Britain by
Cambus Litho, East Kilbride

A FIRST LOOK BOOK

Military Planes

Contents

High-flying Eagle	4
Early fighter planes	6
Air power	8
Jets	10
Modern fighters	12
Jet bombers	14
Guns, missiles, bombs	16
Patrol and recce planes	18
Jump jets	20
Transports	22
Navy planes	24
Tomorrow's air force	26
Plane spotting	28
Glossary	30
Index	32

High-flying Eagle

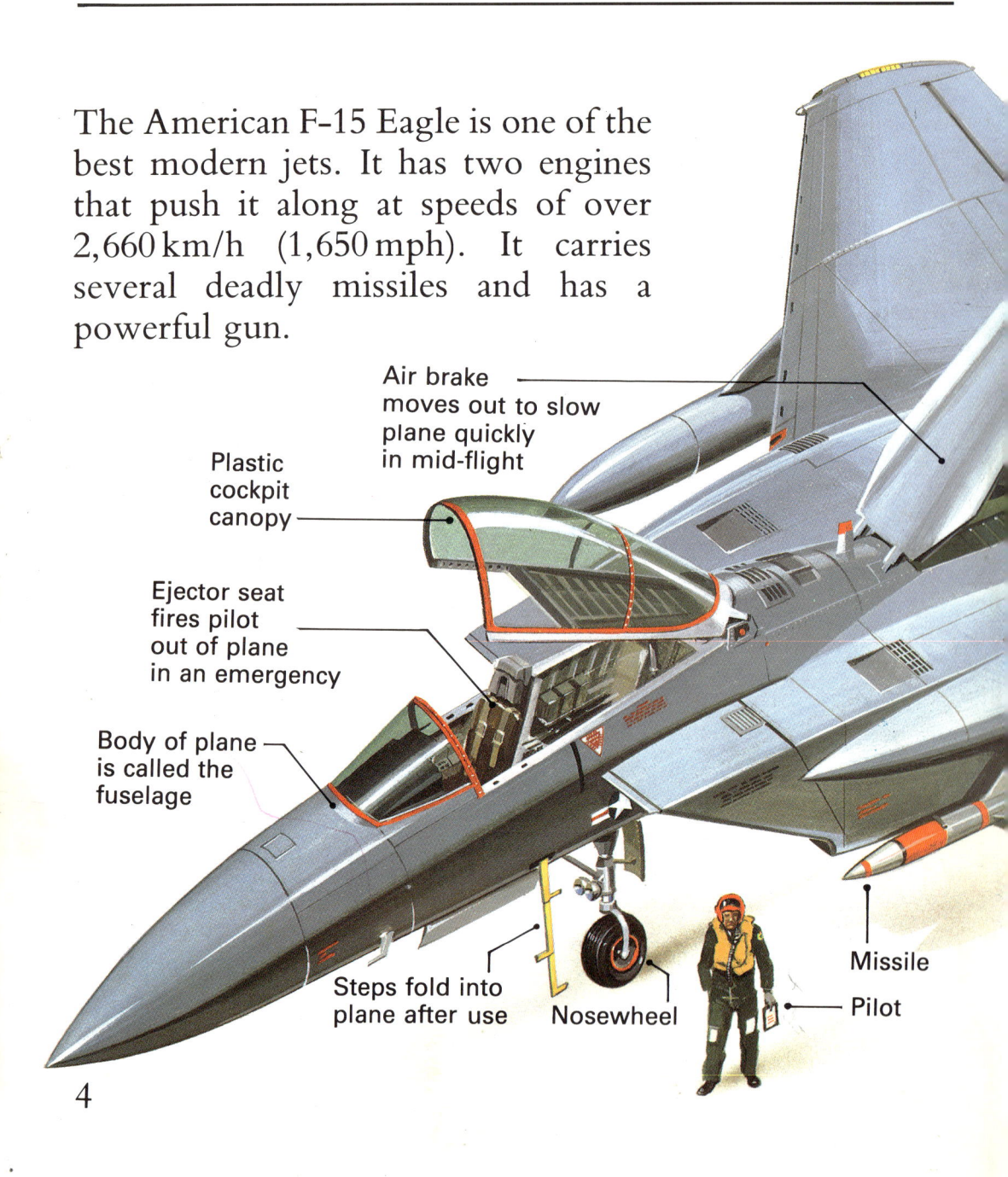

The American F-15 Eagle is one of the best modern jets. It has two engines that push it along at speeds of over 2,660 km/h (1,650 mph). It carries several deadly missiles and has a powerful gun.

Air brake moves out to slow plane quickly in mid-flight

Plastic cockpit canopy

Ejector seat fires pilot out of plane in an emergency

Body of plane is called the fuselage

Steps fold into plane after use

Nosewheel

Missile

Pilot

Two fins keep plane stable in forward flight

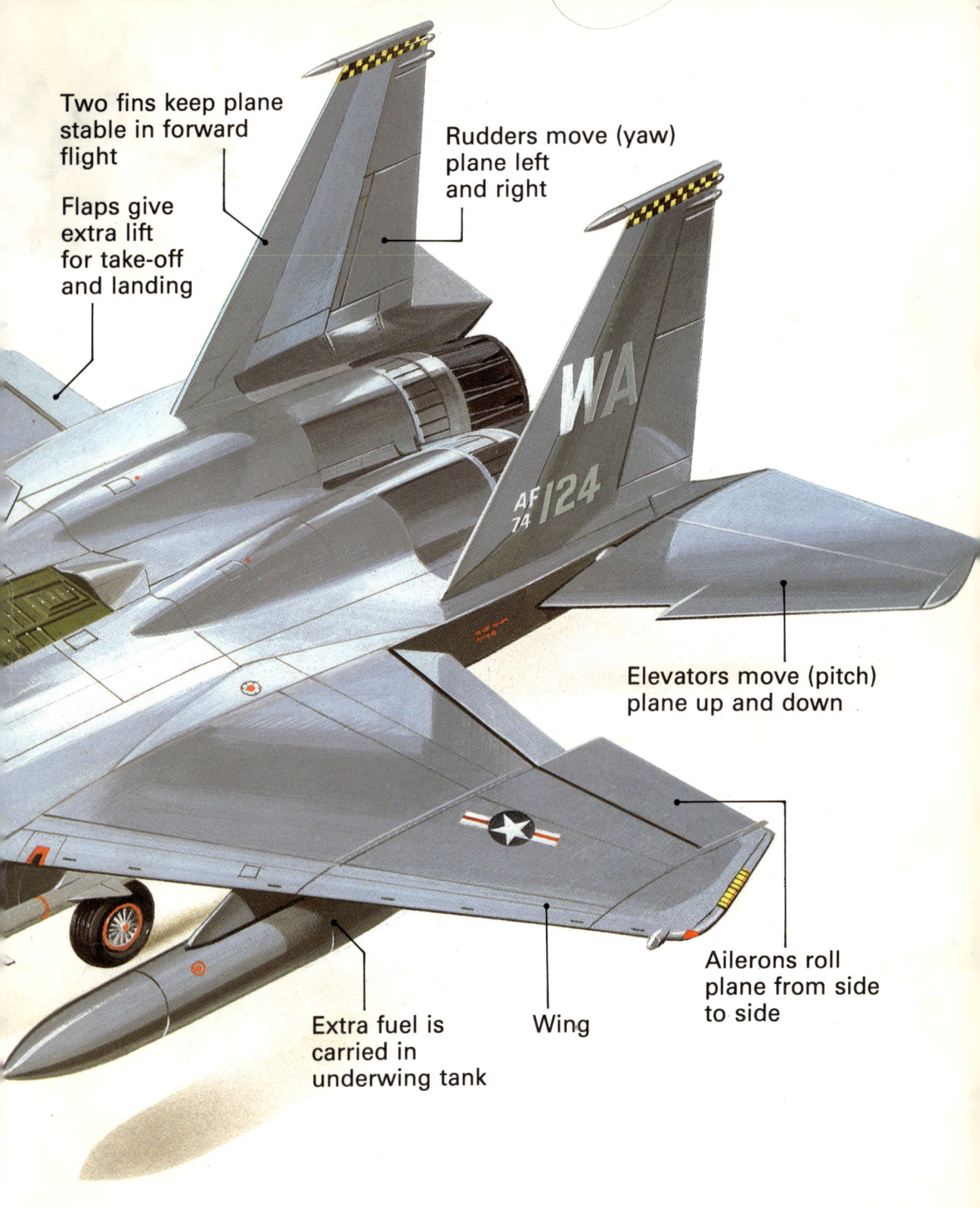

Flaps give extra lift for take-off and landing

Rudders move (yaw) plane left and right

Elevators move (pitch) plane up and down

Ailerons roll plane from side to side

Extra fuel is carried in underwing tank

Wing

5

Early fighter planes

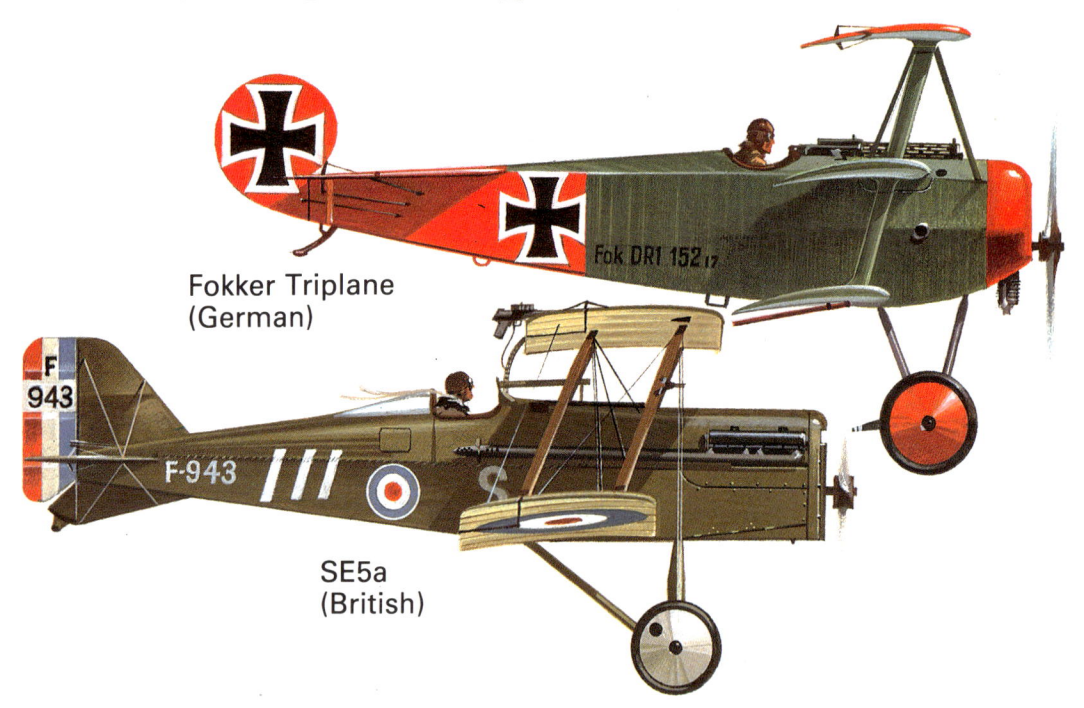

Fokker Triplane
(German)

SE5a
(British)

△ These four fighters were all used in World War I. The Fokker had three wings. The SE5a was one of the best British planes. Many Americans flew in the French-made SPADs. The Hanriot, like most others of the time, was a biplane. It had two wings, one above the other.

The first aerial combats took place over France in World War I. In the earliest combats, known as dogfights, pilots often were armed only with pistols. If the planes carried bombs, they were aimed and dropped by hand. The earliest planes were built as scouts, not fighting machines.

Progress in aircraft design was swift though, and soon planes were being made with powerful engines and

Hanriot HD-1
(Belgian)

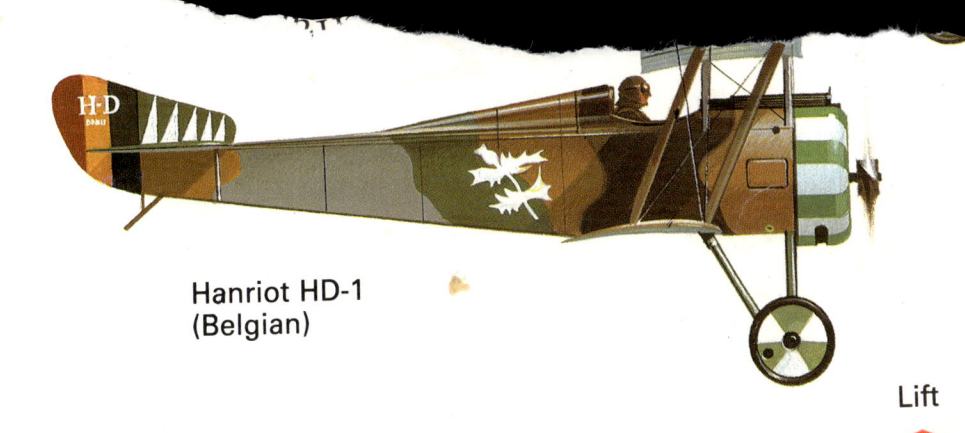

machine guns. The wings and fuselage were made of wood, covered with fabric. There was little or no protection for the pilot against enemy bullets and there was a constant danger of fire. Parachutes had not been invented. If a plane was hit by enemy guns or the engine failed, the pilot went down with the plane. But with luck and skill the pilot could make a forced landing and get out alive.

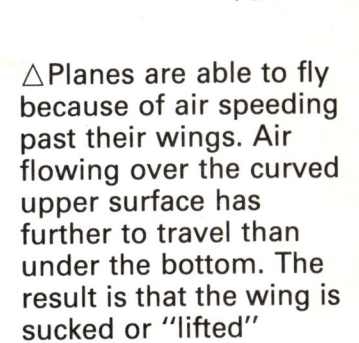

△ Planes are able to fly because of air speeding past their wings. Air flowing over the curved upper surface has further to travel than under the bottom. The result is that the wing is sucked or "lifted" upwards.

over Europe on attack raids. The Fortress was named because of the dozen or more machine guns it carried for protection.

...weapons of ...World War II, bombers were used to attack many cities.

Bomber planes ranged from single seaters, armed with a small bomb under each wing, to huge four-engined planes like the B-17 Flying Fortress shown below. Fortresses flew long missions, escorted by planes such as the P-51D Mustang. Mustangs carried extra fuel under their wings in "drop" tanks to enable them to fly long distances with the bombers. Drop tanks were so-called because they could be dropped in mid-air if necessary. In air combat, the extra weight of fuel tanks could mean the difference between winning or losing a fight.

△ Three famous fighters of World War II. Top to bottom: British Spitfire, German Messerschmitt 109, American P-51D. All could fly at over 580 km/h (350 mph).

Jets

△ The Messerschmitt 262 was the first jet fighter used in battle. The twin-jet could reach 870 km/h (540 mph). Its engines were unreliable though, and many crashed on take-off or landing.

The invention of the jet engine meant that planes could fly higher and faster than ever before. The first jet plane, the Heinkel 178, flew in 1939. A few years later, there were many other jets flying. The great advantage of jet power is speed. The fastest propeller plane has flown at 877 km/h (545 mph). But the world speed record for a jet plane is 3,331 km/h (2,070 mph).

For many years, jet engines were noisy and used far more fuel than propeller planes. Today, jets are quieter, powerful and economical.

How a jet engine works

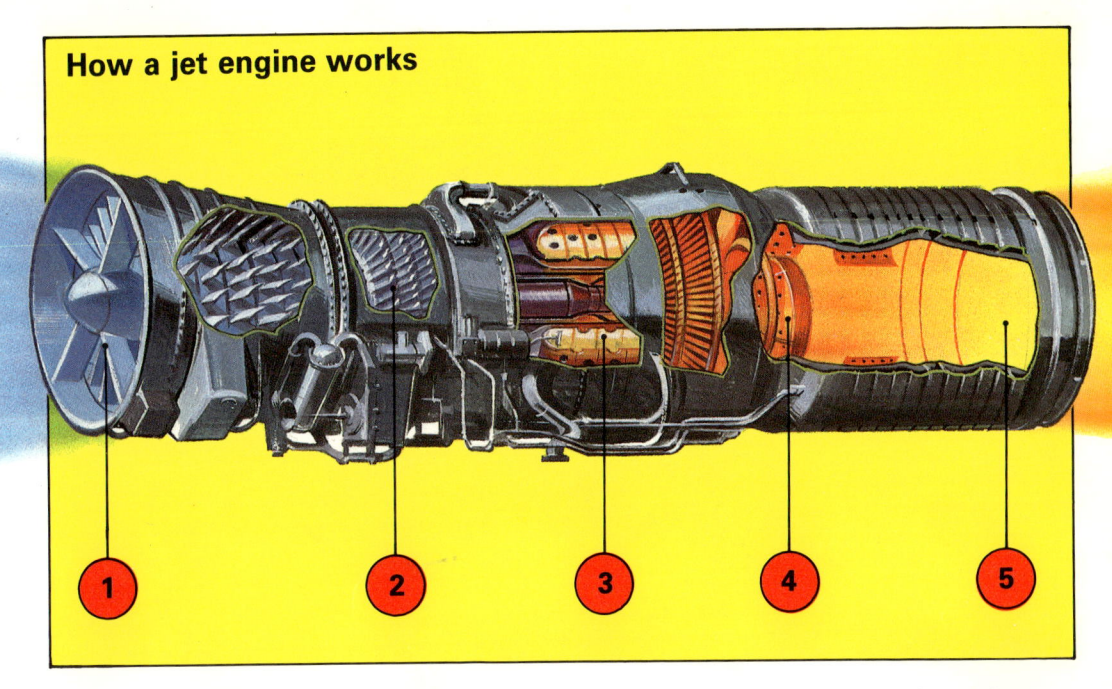

1 2 3 4 5

1 Air is sucked in the front through the air intake.
2 Air is squashed, or compressed, by a series of spinning turbine blades.
3 Fuel is mixed with the air and ignited.
4 Roaring fuel-air mixture rushes out of the exhaust at the back.
5 High-speed jet exhaust pushes engine forward.

▽The P-80 Shooting Star of 1945 was an early American jet. The plane was used for many years and versions of it are still used as trainer planes today.

Modern fighters

△ This picture shows the cockpit of a Grumman F-14 Tomcat interceptor. The F-14 carries up to six Phoenix missiles. They can hit enemy planes over 193 km (120 miles) away. Other missiles and a gun are used for close-in fighting.

Fighters of today are extremely complex. They are expensive to build, costing £20 million or more each.

Computers are essential on board. They help the pilot to use his weapons and to navigate and fly the plane smoothly. But despite the hundreds of knobs, dials and switches, the basic controls are much the same as those of a World War I aircraft.

Mirage 2000

F-16

MiG 21

The rudder is worked by pedals at the pilot's feet. The elevators are moved by the "stick". It is usually in the centre, between the pilot's knees. Moving the stick back and forth makes the elevators pitch the plane's nose up or down so that it can climb or dive. Moving the stick from side to side controls the ailerons. These roll the plane to make it turn.

△ Three modern fighters. The French Mirage 2000 is firing a missile. The US F-16 Fighting Falcon has an air intake under the fuselage. The Russian MiG 21 first entered service in 1958 and is still a popular fighter with over 20 air forces.

13

Jet bombers

△ The B-52 is one of the world's biggest bombers. It has eight engines and a wingspan of 56.4 m (185 ft). It can carry various attack missiles or a bomb load of over 31 tonnes.

The job of these planes is to transport a war-load over enemy territory and to drop bombs precisely on target.

Bombers used to fly very high, out of reach of ground defences. But modern missiles make such high-flying attacks almost impossible. Today's bombers all fly the last part of their attack route as low as possible. Ground-hugging flights make it difficult for defence radars to spot a plane. This leaves little time for missiles to be fired at the bomber.

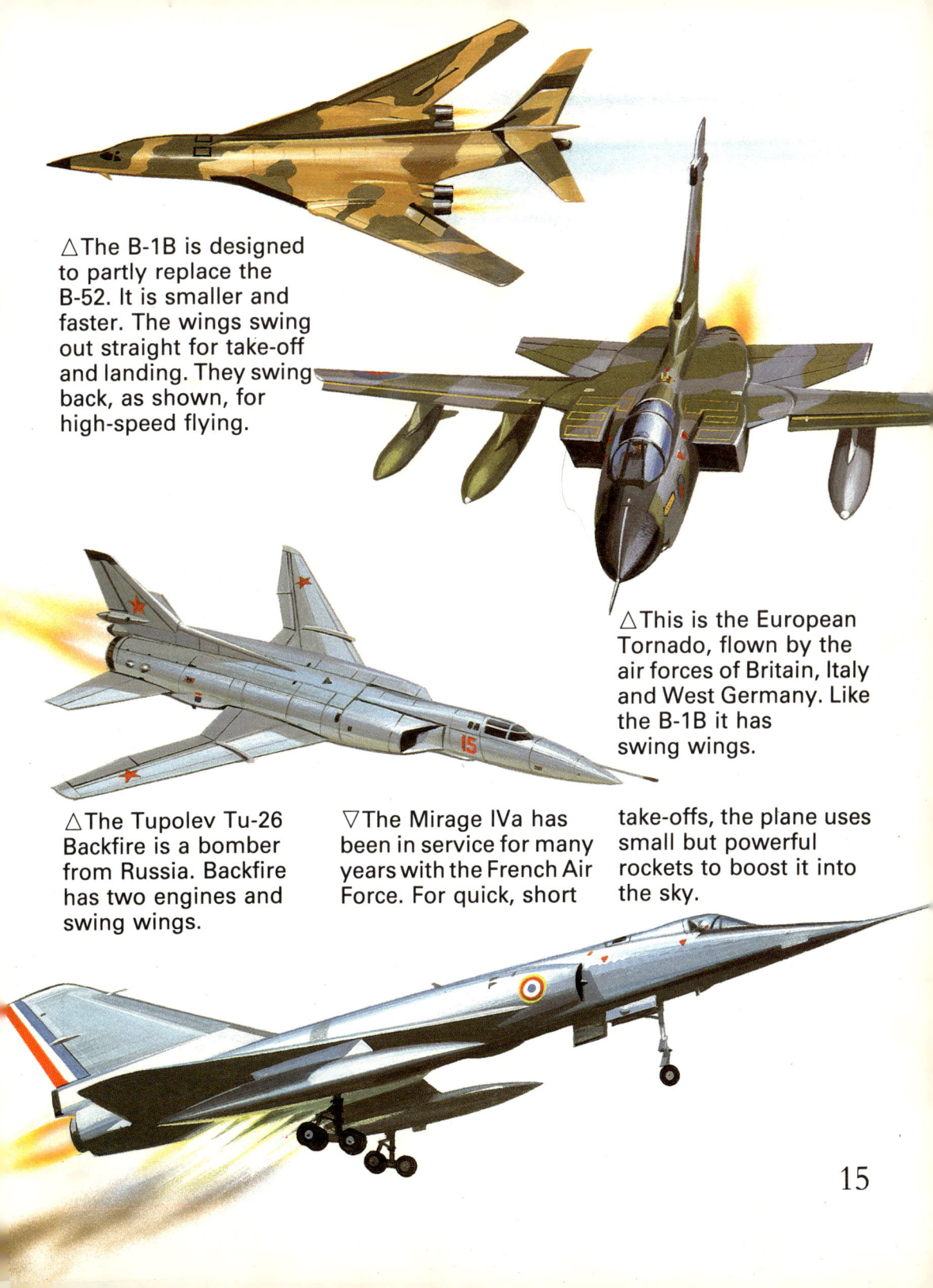

△The B-1B is designed to partly replace the B-52. It is smaller and faster. The wings swing out straight for take-off and landing. They swing back, as shown, for high-speed flying.

△This is the European Tornado, flown by the air forces of Britain, Italy and West Germany. Like the B-1B it has swing wings.

△The Tupolev Tu-26 Backfire is a bomber from Russia. Backfire has two engines and swing wings.

▽The Mirage IVa has been in service for many years with the French Air Force. For quick, short take-offs, the plane uses small but powerful rockets to boost it into the sky.

15

Guns, missiles, bombs

△ Modern jets can carry a huge variety of weapons. Here a Jaguar displays the sort of weapons it can carry. They range from small rockets to bombs that can destroy runways. The Jaguar cannot carry everything shown here at the same time though!

Most fighting planes still have guns, though cannon have replaced machine guns in most cases. Cannon shells are bigger, and so cause more damage.

There are missiles made for every possible purpose. Small missiles such as the Sidewinder are used in air combat. Missiles such as the French Exocet are built for the anti-ship role.

Ordinary "iron bombs" are still used, though many have steering vanes and are guided by laser beams.

Tank-busting GAU-8
The GAU-8 gun shown here is one of the most powerful in the world. It can fire over 4,000 shells a minute. The weapon is especially useful against tanks. The force of its attack can smash through thick armour.

Heat-seeking Sidewinder missile
The Sidewinder is a lightweight missile used for attacking other planes in air combat. It has a heat-sensitive detector in its nose. This guides the missile towards the hot engine exhaust of the enemy plane.

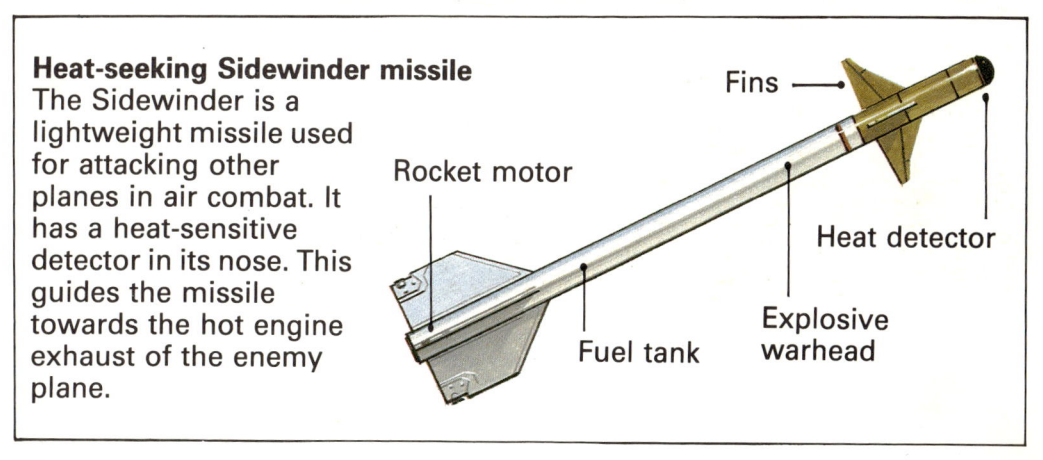

Fins
Rocket motor
Heat detector
Fuel tank
Explosive warhead

Ship-killing Exocet
This missile can be fired many kilometres away from a ship. Once fired, it guides itself automatically, flying just above the waves.

Patrol and recce planes

△Patrol planes like this British Aerospace Nimrod fly over oceans for up to 12 hours at a time. They have detectors to spot enemy ships or submarines. Nimrods also keep watch over lonely areas such as the North Sea oil rig shown above. If a ship sinks or is lost, Nimrods search to find any surviving sailors.

Patrol planes fly long, lonely flights over large areas. They keep a look-out for the enemy. Overland flights check for troop or tank movements on the ground. Ocean flights keep watch for ships or submarines. Both missions look out for enemy aircraft too. If an aircraft is spotted, an interceptor is sent up to investigate.

Ocean patrollers such as the Nimrod, shown above, are equipped with many weapons to attack enemy

Lockheed TR-1

Lockheed SR-71

Tupolev Bear

vessels. It carries mines, missiles and torpedoes.

Reconnaissance ("recce") planes are built to fly over enemy territory, taking photographs of secret installations, such as missile bases. Some, such as the Lockheed TR-1, fly slowly. The Lockheed also flies extremely high to avoid being spotted. Superfast jets like the SR-71 rely on flying faster than any missiles which may be sent to attack them.

△ Three very different patrol planes. The TR-1 is a glider-like single seater, used to keep watch over battlefields. Russian Bears were once used as bombers. Now they are used for long distance patrols. The SR-71 is the world's fastest plane. It can fly at over 3,220 km/h (2,000 mph).

Jump jets

△Here you see a pair of Sea Harriers, ready for an attack mission. They are shown carrying bombs and Sidewinder missiles.

Jump jets are planes that can take off and land vertically, so they do not need a runway. The British Harrier is the best known.

The Harrier has a single engine, with four swivelling nozzles, two either side of the fuselage. For take-off, they point down, so that jet thrust lifts the plane off the ground. Once airborne, the pilot slowly swivels the nozzles backwards. Soon the plane is flying at

Vertical take-off

Jet nozzles point downwards

Forward flight

Jet nozzles point rearwards

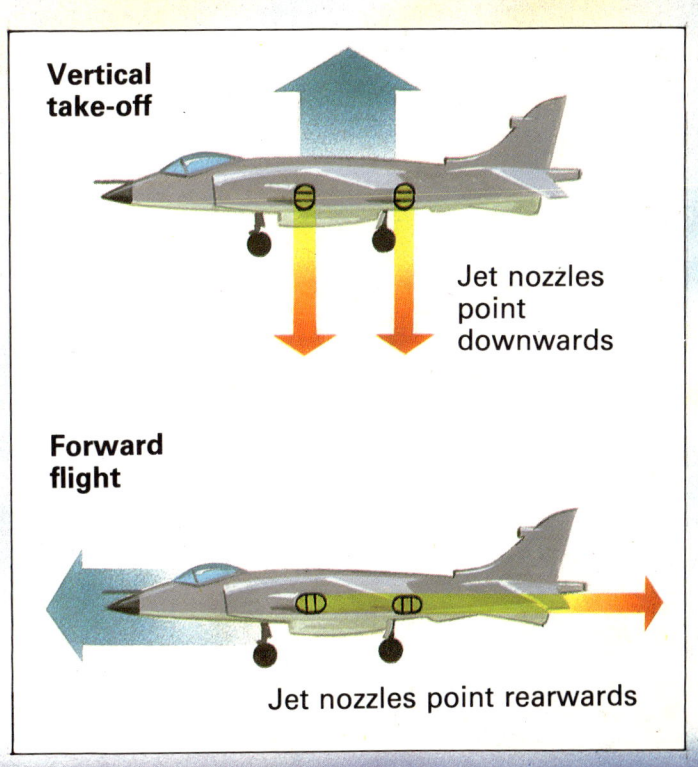

speeds of up to 1,200 km/h (745 mph).

In air combat, the Harrier can be one of the most manoeuvrable planes in the world. Its pilot can swivel the jet nozzles in mid-flight to brake, dodge and accelerate the plane.

The Sea Harriers shown above are built for navy use. They are carried aboard small aircraft carriers. Sea Harriers have a raised cockpit so the pilot has a good all round view.

△ This diagram shows how a Harrier jump-jet works. The jet nozzles point downwards for vertical take-off and landing. For forward flight they swivel back to thrust the plane along.

21

Transports

△ The mighty C-5A is powered by four huge jet engines.

▽ This cross-section of a C-5A shows the huge cargo bay which can carry tanks, jeeps, helicopters and other equipment.

All air forces use transport planes. They carry passengers, heavy cargo and weapons.

The C-5A, shown above, is one of the biggest cargo planes. It has 28 landing wheels, which enable it to take off and land on short, rough airstrips. It can carry over 100 tonnes of cargo. This may include two tanks or up to three big helicopters!

The Hercules, shown on the right, is widely used. It is flown by the air forces of more than 40 countries. It can fly from short, rough airstrips.

▽The Lockheed Hercules is a popular four-engined transport plane.
1 Big flight deck
2 Cargo bay
3 Four engines
4 Loading ramp swings down so that vehicles can be driven in.

△For easy loading, the C-5A's nose swings up. Here you see a DSRV mini-submarine going aboard. It is designed to save sailors trapped in damaged submarines on the seabed.

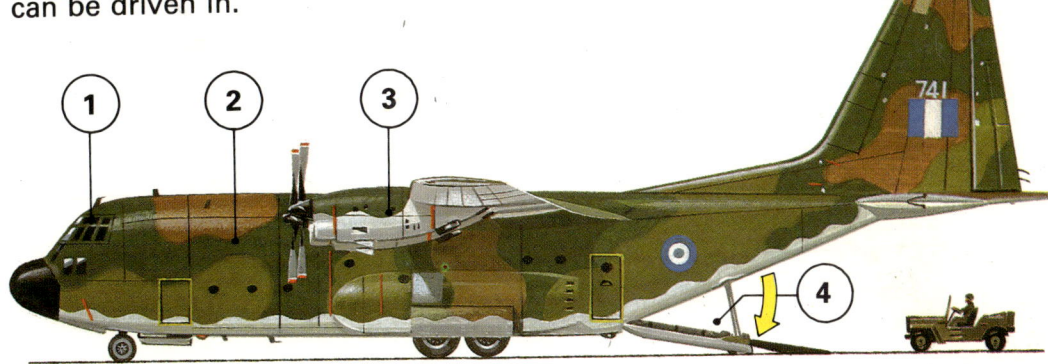

23

Navy planes

F-14 Tomcat

Super Etendard

△ The French Super Etendard is an attack plane. It often carries the Exocet anti-ship missile. The F-14 Tomcat is a two-seater interceptor. It is armed with up to six long-range missiles and four Sidewinders. It has swing wings.

Navy planes are built for use aboard aircraft carriers. Aircraft are fired into the air by steam-powered catapults. When an aircraft lands, its wheels slam on to the deck. The plane's arrester hook catches one of several wires across the deck. The arrester wire hauls the plane to a halt in a few metres.

Both landing and take-off require great skill, particularly when the carrier is pitching and rolling through the waves in rough weather.

▽The Prowler flies with bomber formations. It carries electronic equipment to confuse and jam enemy defences. The F-18 Hornet is a new navy plane. Both fighter and bomber versions are made.

△Here you see operations aboard the flight deck of the USS *Nimitz* aircraft carrier. An F-14 Tomcat is ready for take-off.

F-18 Hornet

EA6B Prowler

25

△ This is the Grumman X-29. It is the first fighter plane to be built with forward sweep wings. It will be used for test flights.

26

Tomorrow's air force

Here you see planes that may be flying in years to come.

New materials will enable forward sweep wings to be made. These wings should make combat planes even more agile. A rounded shape is difficult for radar to spot, making it ideal for bombers which need to sneak into enemy territory.

△ "Flying bat" aircraft like this could be flying by 1990. The curved wing gives lots of low-speed lift for take-off and landing.

Plane spotting

△ To catch a plane as it flies by, swing the camera with it as you press the shutter. This plane is a Hawker Hart of the 1930s.

The best place to see a range of military aircraft is at an air show.

If you take your camera, you should be able to get some interesting pictures. Unless you have a telephoto lens, it is best to concentrate on parked aircraft, where you can get close to them. Pictures of planes in the air all too often result in a tiny blurred shape. Make a note of any interesting markings so that you can keep a record.

◁Look out for planes with unusual markings. You can use the pictures as reference for model-making. This is a T-33, the trainer version of the P-80 shown on page 11.

▽Keep your eyes open for close-up pictures. Here a member of the ground crew inspects a Harvard trainer.

△Look around inside aircraft hangars if you can. Here, a Fokker Triplane is being made as good as new some 70 years after its first flight.

29

Glossary

Here is a list of some of the technical words used in this book.

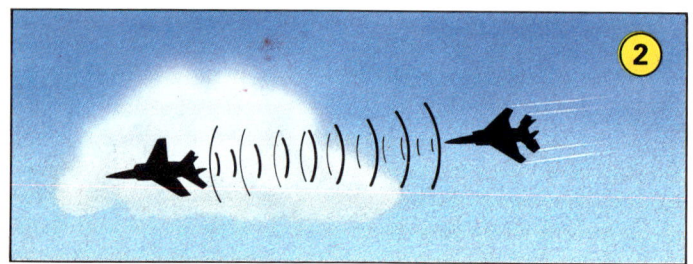

△ Radar is used on most planes as a form of early warning system. The diagram above shows how it works.
1 Plane sends out a radio wave from its radar dish in the nose cone.
2 The radio wave bounces off any solid object, such as the enemy aircraft, shown hidden in cloud. The radar dish receives the bounced "echo". The signal is displayed as a glowing blob on a TV screen in the cockpit instrument panel.

Flight deck
The flat top of an aircraft carrier, where planes take off and land.

Forward sweep
Most planes have their wings swept *back*. Forward sweep is the exact opposite. Experimental planes are being built using new carbon-fibre materials. These can stand the increased strain forward-sweep wings undergo in flight.

Jamming
Word used to describe electronic interference. The Grumman Prowler carries lots of jamming equipment to confuse enemy defence radars, missiles and aircraft.

Laser
Needle-thin beam of intense light. Used by some aircraft as a type of bomb and missile aiming device. An attacking plane shines a laser beam on a target. The bomb or missile homes in on the spot of laser light to hit the target dead on.

Stick

Pilot's term for the control column. Movement of the stick moves the elevators and ailerons. Firing buttons for guns and missiles are usually on the stick too. It is usually positioned between the pilot's legs. Some planes, such as the F-16, have a side stick. This is mounted on the side of the cockpit. The pilot can hold the stick without taking his arm off the arm rest. This makes control of the plane easier.

Swing wing

Type of wing which swings out straight for take-off and landing, then sweeps back for high-speed flight. Straight wings give more lift, making take-offs shorter. Swept wings cut through the air more smoothly, making top speeds higher. Some aircraft, such as the F-14, have automatic wing sweep controlled by computers. The Tornado has manual control – the pilot is in charge of the sweep angle.

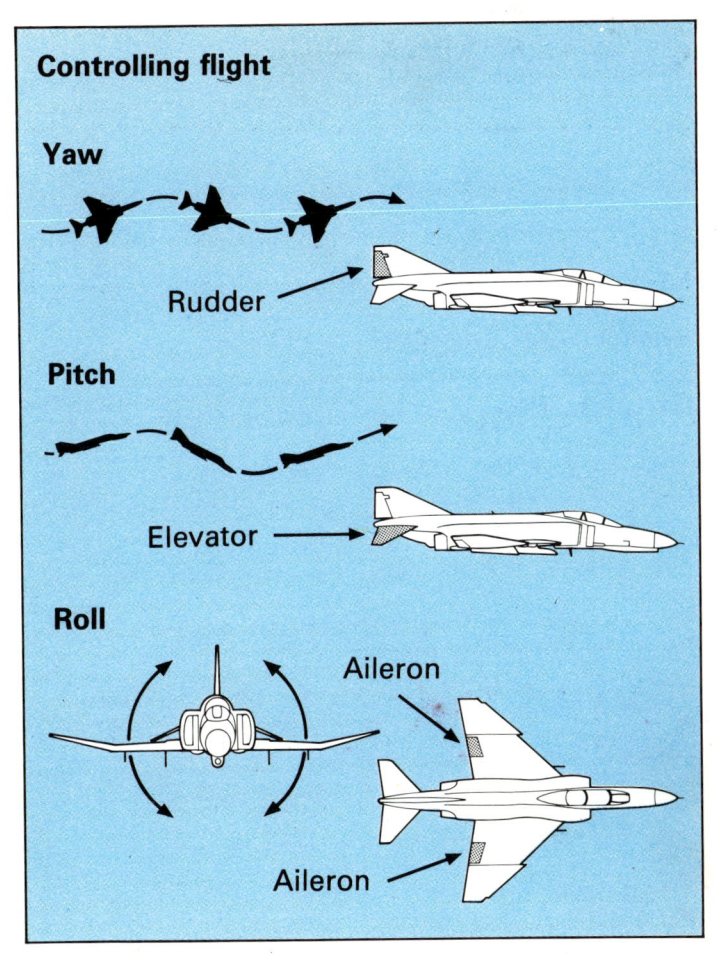

Controlling flight

Yaw

Pitch

Roll

△ These pictures show the way in which the various controls affect a plane's flight path. The rudder swings the plane from side to side. This is called yaw. The elevators move the plane nose up or down. This is called pitch. The ailerons move the plane in a rolling motion.

Flight controls may be manual or power-assisted, so that small amounts of pressure from the pilot's hands and feet work the controls.
The plane shown in the diagrams is an F-4 Phantom II, one of the most successful fighters built in the 1970s.

31

Index

ailerons, 5, 13, 31
aircraft carriers, 20, 24, 25, 30

B-1B, 15
B-17, 8, 9
B-52, 14, 15
biplane, 6
bomber planes, 8, 14

C-5A, 22, 23
cannon, 16

dogfights, 6
drop tanks, 9

Eagle, American F-15, 4
elevators, 5, 13, 31
Etendard, 24
Exocet, 16, 17, 24

F-4 Phantom II, 31
F-14 Tomcat, 12, 24, 25, 31
F-15, 4
F-16 Fighting Falcon, 13, 31
F-18 Hornet, 25
flight deck, 25, 30
"Flying bat", 27
Flying Fortress, 8, 9
Fokker, 6, 29
forward sweep, 27, 30

GAU-8 gun, 17

Hanriot HD-1, 6, 7, 17
Harrier, 20, 21
Hawker Hart, 28
Heinkel 178, 10
Hercules, 22, 23
Hornet, 25

Jaguar, 16
jamming, 30
jet engine, 10, 11
jump jets, 20, 21

laser beam, 16, 30

Messerschmitt 109, 9
Messerschmitt 262, 10
MiG 21, 13
Mirage IVa, 15
Mirage 2000, 13
Mustang, 9

Nimrod, 18

P-51D Mustang, 9
P-80, 11, 29
Phantom II, 31
Phoenix missiles, 12
pitch, 5, 13, 31
Prowler, 25, 30

radar, 14, 30
reconnaissance, 19
roll, 4, 13, 31
rudder, 5, 13, 31
Russian Bear, 19

SE5a, 6
Sea Harrier, 20, 21
Shooting Star P-80, 11
Sidewinder, 16, 17, 20, 24
SPAD X111, 6, 7
Spitfire, 9
SR-71, 18, 19
stick (control column), 13, 31
sweep wings, 26, 27, 31
swing wings, 15, 31

T-33, 29
Tomcat, 12, 24, 25, 31
Tornado, 15, 31
TR-1, 18, 19
triplane, 6, 29
Tupolev Tu-26 Backfire, 15
twin jet, 10

USS *Nimitz*, 25

world's fastest plane, 19
world speed records, 10
World War I, 6, 12
World War II, 8, 9, 12

X-29, 26

yaw, 5, 31

32